Escape of Light

poems by

Deborah Kahan Kolb

Finishing Line Press
Georgetown, Kentucky

Dedicated to my blessings: Yossi and Alyssa, Joshua, Kayla, Daniel, Eden—and most of all, to Tom, for the countless openings you've created for trapped light to escape.

Escape of Light

"...black holes ain't as black as they are painted. They are not the eternal prisons they were once thought. Things can get out of a black hole, both to the outside and possibly to another universe. So if you feel you are in a black hole, don't give up. There's a way out."
—Stephen Hawking

"There is a crack in everything/That's how the light gets in..."
—Leonard Cohen (from "Anthem")

Copyright © 2020 by Deborah Kahan Kolb
ISBN 978-1-64662-150-7 First Edition
All rights reserved under International and Pan-American Copyright Conventions. No part of this book may be reproduced in any manner whatsoever without written permission from the publisher, except in the case of brief quotations embodied in critical articles and reviews.

ACKNOWLEDGMENTS

I'm grateful to the editors of the journals and magazines in which the following poems first appeared, some with slight revisions:

3Elements Review: "Psalm for a Son's Burial"
Art Kibbutz "Wonder Woman" reading at NYC Poetry Festival: "you the shining thing"
Literary Mama: "Grandmommy"
Lunch Ticket: "How to Leave the Girl Behind" (excerpted from the story "Red Bird Rising")
Mom Egg Review: "Emerging, Art of"
New Verse News: "Lullaby for Charlottesville" (as "Charlottesville: A Cautionary Tale")
New Verse News; Rise Up Review: "Spectrum: November 8, 2016"
Paddock Review: "Au Pair"
Poets Reading the News; Writers Resist: "The Big Top Comes Down"
PRISM: An Interdisciplinary Journal for Holocaust Educators: "Re(vision)"
Tuck Magazine: "Brandenburg Gate," "The Woman in the Ring"
Voices Israel Anthology; Shirim Journal: "After Auschwitz"

"After Auschwitz" and "Re(vision)" have been adapted for the short film *Write Me* (Dir. Pearl Gluck. Perf. Lynn Cohen. Palinka Pictures/Pintele Productions, 2019).

"What Lies Within" first appeared as "The Cusp" in *Windows and a Looking Glass* (Finishing Line Press, 2017).

"you the shining thing" is inspired by women who love women, women whose freedom is born of lies, women who must sometimes bury their former selves in order to live authentic lives. To these women I offer wedding bells of a different sort. Dedicated to T. and N.

Publisher: Leah Maines
Editor: Christen Kincaid
Cover Art: Thomas Kolb
Author Photo: Alona Cohen Photography
Cover Design: Elizabeth Maines McCleavy

Printed in the USA on acid-free paper.
Order online: www.finishinglinepress.com
　　　　　also available on amazon.com

Author inquiries and mail orders:
Finishing Line Press
P. O. Box 1626
Georgetown, Kentucky 40324
U. S. A.

Table of Contents

Emerging, Art of 1
The Gestures of Trees 2
The Woman in the Ring 3
Grandmommy 5
My Son's Gay Twin 6
Au Pair 7
What Lies Within 9
How to Leave the Girl Behind 10
Re(vision) 11
After Auschwitz 12
Brandenburg Gate 14
Showering at the Swiss Hotel 15
Spectrum: November 8, 2016 16
Lullaby for Charlottesville 17
Psalm for a Son's Burial 18
I Consider Forty 21
He Wonders What It's Like to be Pregnant 22
you the shining thing 23
The Women are the Story 25
First Date 26
East, Meet West 27
An Unusual Collection 28
The Secret Real Life of Anon 30
Excess 31
The Big Top Comes Down: A Consciousness Poem 34
Jessica Rabbit Plays the Piano 35

Emerging, Art of

Check the box that best describes
your career thus far, the form says, or how you see
yourself as a writer.

It seems I've been emerging
for a number of years now. But how do I see
myself—tunneling down the dark fleshy corridor
of my mother's cervix covered in ick, my slippery
soft skull bones mashed, intent on the drowning
sounds and the wreath of light ahead, finally emerging
to my first strident yawp?
And from that moment hence the steady
march of metamorphosis,
of emerging and becoming.

What must the torpid caterpillar do to emerge
from its glistening chrysalis a laurel-crowned monarch?
The worm digests itself. The lowly pupa
writes itself off in hopes of emerging
a butterfly laureate.
Self-immolation, it seems, is a requirement
for emerging.

So when you knock at the majestic doors, be prepared
for bleeding knuckles and a tamped
down spirit, be prepared to extinguish
yourself in a phoenix fire before you can emerge.
Established.

The Gestures of Trees

I imagine it must be Godlike to create
something from nothing. Sound
from silence.
The stealthy escape of light

from the tight black hole of space.

The close wrapped buds on the magnolia tree
outside my newborn daughter's window wave
and beckon shyly,
resurrected from their snow-

shrouds, the frozen decay that birthed them.

Come out to play, little girl.
Like you, we were only a figment last season.
And now we live.

The Woman in the Ring

was clearly celebrating
something.
Life. Or the abdication of
care.
To my eight year old
eyes
she was glorious, a
rainbow
swathed in chieftain
feathers,
a glistening Santa Fe
turquoise
nestled in the silver
filigree
of her throat's dusky
hollow.

When she laughed her bright teeth
moonbeamed from her brown mouth but
my mama said I must be dreaming.
When she swirled her frayed skirts
frolicked with her shining calves but
my mama said it was time to grow up.
When she beckoned with a crooked finger
cracked long ago by the rage of a large man
my mama said *stop yo' nonsense now*

I was in thrall to the
cottony dread-
locks snaking down her bony back
wrapped in a gleaming
band of sun-
shine, to the glint of gold
peeping between
her tinseled toe-

nails, and I never noticed
the blackened fissures
of her cracked heel, or her
scabby pale palm,
or our matching meta-
skin.

Grandmommy

Because you stayed silent you took
                        the newborn child downy and slick,
soaked with her mother's rage,
howling with your daughter's grief,
                        you took her as yours and imagined
that you bore down, veins engorged purple,
scarlet carnations blossoming from your
                        capillaries and sweat-pools streaming
from your taut temples and you
believed that you bore her yourself,
                        birthed your own granddaughter,
how does that even make sense, but
you made sense of it rather than bear
                        the terrible knowing of your silence
while he sinned her dreams away,
not even a sin you can name but
                        the unthinkable *allowing* of things
to unfold, and your teenage daughter
barely able to bear the nine months
                        of swelling silence, of a scarlet
secret hiding in the hush that
begins and ends with a bloody gush,
                        growing even as her belly grew
a life she felt was a death and
you were impotent with silence,
                        feeble in the face of this history—
a baby having a baby having
a baby having a baby and so
                        the burden of birth is passed
from grandmother to mother to
daughter to grandmother and so
                        because you stayed silent
she called you Grandmommy,
a one-person-all-mixed-up.

My Son's Gay Twin

I met today my son's gay twin, a man
whom I never pushed screaming from my body.
An idea—until that moment I stepped

into the shop on Main selling lush dreams and lavender
scented air, when he grinned and called me "sweetie."
Bizarre, that. Alternate universe stuff,

to see on his face my own face. And how
is it possible for anyone to be so goddamned
impossibly happy. And gay. Some of my best friends

are gay. *Yes, but if he was your own?* The great
unanswerable question—until that moment I stepped
into the shop on Main selling fragrant promises

to dial back time. "My name's Charlie." Charming
young man. I wish I had a son like him. Oh wait,
but in fact I do. On one face, horn rims hint

at bookishness. On the spitting image, green eyes blaze
ambition. On one millennial head, locks close
cropped as befits a man who chases his name

with a degree. And here, a glossy thatch of springtime bends
over a hunk of homemade seaweed soap, wrapping and taping
a smile to be born in this bubble in time.

Au Pair

I.
A cape starling or amethyst, some little bird—
Afrikaans
warbler, shows up in the greening spring, miniature

flicker-beat fluffing her breast, and gingerly finds
her perch among
our young. From somewhere within the murmuration

she exhales, violet-backed, wearing her mantle
like a boy.
Pied starling, fledging along with our own nestlings,

content to hover, and admire the view. Long-tailed
glossy starling,
her plumage lambent and glowing. *Lamprotornis—*

how fitting. A Tiffany work of art. Shimmer
up to us,
little bird. Gently she lights upon our New York

nest, but every so often I sense the sudden
run, the nimble
lift-off and vanishing flight of this lovely bird

back to Port Elizabeth, to the African
nesting ground,
the vivid southern tropics that'd spawned this chick.

II.
No address in the U.S. is proof
of residency except for your pulsing
heart emoji, fitted into a cage
of ribs built of pipe cleaners and hair

elastics, a rainbow of chortles,
and a compass pointing straight ahead

and a little to the left. *Ons is werklik geseënd...*[1]

---

[1] We are truly blessed. (Afrikaans)

What Lies Within

layers
                    like nesting matryoshka dolls
elaborately painted   meticulously decorated
      charming, ornamental…
                    Without obscuring within.
Art as life and so on.
          a spit-shined toy, collectible figurine
                her father carefully handcrafted
     with primitive tools
to gift a prospective bridegroom
                    …oohs and aahs
          flowers and fairy tales…

she's eighteen, almost
    almost old enough   to split
      almost young enough   to sob

      dig
   deep
enough
   if you care to find
      the modesty of the king's child
Dig deep.
      And when your spade strikes
          the slab of light you'll know you've found
   the true daughter,
   the real sister,
   the genuine granddaughter
the
smallest
girl masquerading
          as   the   largest
                                  woman

How to Leave the Girl Behind

Becoming yourself means leave-taking, means reinventing, means self-immolating. You mean to fight your way out of your rigid, glistening chrysalis. You digest the worm that is your self and from the soup you pull your eyes, newly sighted, and wings, antennae. Becoming yourself means flying, means running, means rounding corner after cutting corner, means slamming. Slamming doors that shut fast on the past and open up to poetry and song. You wrench words from somewhere deep. Words explode onto your page, words burst from your lips. Words buried in vaults, words hidden in hollows of shame, words that air the soil of secrets to the cleansing light of day. Words that reignite your mother's distress, your father's wrath, your sisters' rage. Disappointment and dishonor all around. You write lyrics to rap songs, staccato punches that reverberate with anger, sorrow, truth. You write poems of anguish and celebration. You slam in dark dodgy East Village basements. You write torch songs that fuse the fiction of your imagination and the reality of your torn, almost beautiful life. You sing in Bowery lounges that stink of beer and the press of flesh. You sing, you test your brand new wings. You write. You write like you're running out of time, like you're Alexander Hamilton reimagining your country from ground zero up. You build a world. You put the pieces of the broken one back together. You are mother. You are partner. You are nightingale. You are red bird rising, leaving ashes at your feet.

Re(vision)

An old man I know—a great grandfather—
steps into the tattoo parlor, tells the artist,
I am ready to begin my life.

Eight lingering decades carried in his creased cheeks.
Five blue numerals etched in his crinkled skin.
He presents his forearm for erasure.

Make it disappear, the old man says.
This number does not define me.

After Auschwitz

I am vague I am hazy I am indistinct

I am bodiless—
but my black Romani blood river runs
boils and bubbles and
pushes up Piotr's daisies
I am faceless—
but my non-Aryan features glow searing hot
my crippled mouth and communist eyes
coal to cinder
fuel to Himmler's furnaces
the fog of my Jewish bones
blurs Wladyslaw's farmhouse
my homosexual tongue a licking lapping flame
a hideous gape, a burning yawning mask
my embers smolder in the wake of the Zyklon B
that fumigated my lungs
and left me breathless, voiceless, mute.
Silent.

…so I am nameless…
I am vague I am hazy I am indistinct

Write me, Paul Celan
            —your neighbor from Czernowitz
Write me, Nelly Sachs
            —your neighbor from Berlin
Write me, Miklós Radnóti
            —your neighbor from Budapest

Give me a body and fill me in and grant me life.
Birth me—
for oblivion awaits
Birth me—
lest I disappear
from the awareness of humanity
into the amnesia of history
…vapor and ash…

Adorno was wrong—there must be poetry.
Write me.

Brandenburg Gate

Is it fixed now—
now that a flag of light, of blue and of white,
wraps itself around the Brandenburg Gate

> because four Jewish soldiers on a Jerusalem corner were crushed
> into the world to come by a truck blind with hate?

In 1939 crimson flags billow and bleed
beneath the columns of the Brandenburg Gate,
adorned with marching black swastikas, like twisted tarantulas
who exterminate their living prey.

Unter den Linden is now a street, was once a song
your Bubbe hummed
to her long ago babies in a dying tongue,
her Yiddish not so very unlike the German they spit
to the goosestep and drum
behind bolted synagogue doors just as they lit

> up the pyres of Jews; and the SS helmets then darkened
> her doorstep and made a memory of her four Jewish births.

In 2017 the Brandenburg Gate is lit up in brilliant
blue and white with a six-pointed star—not yellow
this time, not howling Jude, but still announcing to the world
the slaughter of Jews.

Showering at the Swiss Hotel

IN THE NEWS: *Outrage erupted [Tuesday] after a small Swiss hotel posted a sign asking "Jewish guests" to shower before using the swimming pool.*

To our Jewish guests:
Tell your daughter, tell your son

to shower before swimming
        in our pale pale pool;

to abstain from playing
        on our white sand beach;

to refrain from breathing
        our pure pure air.

You understand, dear guest, neutral is no more.

We are obliged to prevent
                      your   stain
                                from   spreading.

Spectrum: November 8, 2016

The day the red-ones drew the curtains and chose the orange-one
to mind the white oval that had embraced the black-one
nearly three thousand days—that day

was the day the blue-ones formed
a veined parenthesis to contain the pulsing mass
of the red-ones, spilling sideways,

was the day the red-ones and the blue-ones
never turned to purple and the green-ones
stayed scattered, shoots pushing up to be counted,

was the day the brown-ones huddled and burst, and
waited for the white-ones, the eye-holed pointed ones,
to bear a burning broken cross, its twisted arms akimbo,

was the day the pink-ones, like the blue-one who
missed her grip at the finish, snatched steel from
between their legs and bound themselves each to each,

was the day the tan-ones veiled themselves
into invisibility,

was the day the yellow-ones shifted, and strove
for the exits,

was the day the beige-ones bent double, and breathed
dios mio,

was the day the rainbows clung together, their colors melted
and shriven,

was the day a keening *Hallelujah* rose up from the teeming streets
and evanesced into the violet sky,

was the day I waited for the raging ones to bring a yellow star
for me.

Lullaby for Charlottesville

The Nazis have returned. To Charlottesville, VA.
      Pale wizards, frenzied mass, mad with purity.
Wands ablaze, heads of skin, howling blood and soil.

Tell your Jewish son. Repeat the story. Pray.
      Tell him he will never replace the whiteness of their line.
He will never replace never replace the blood pooled in the soil.

Tell your son the truth about the trains of yesterday.
      When children came in cattle cars and left as clouds of ash.
When memories were skin, bones, weeping bloody soil.

In Charlottesville the torches turn the nighttime into day.
      Long ago these torches fired ovens for the Jews.
Step-children of goose-steppers want blood spilled on their soil.

Tell your Jewish daughter. Find the words to say
      They are raging to destroy her with fire and a flag.
Swear never again never again. No more blood for soil.

      Now you've told the story that bears repeating every day.
You've told your son. Now try to drain the olive from his skin.
You've told your daughter. Try to drain the darkness from her hair,
      Fix the hook that is her nose. Bury the blood lost in the soil.

Psalm for a Son's Burial
(in memoriam B.D.)

Hush now, it must be written somewhere
that death is the domain of men.

The father, spent, eulogizes the son—
or the brother, the husband—and he knows his time

for sleep is done. They grab the shovels
and empty the last of the balm of hurt minds

into the void, then they cover your heartbeat
in a silence broken by a rustle and chuff,
the men.

And somewhere, too, it must be written
that birth is the domain of women.

The mother who conceived and carried
and birthed you in blood shakes—the vessel

whose cracks have yawned into fissures
splits wide open, her center cannot hold,

her head shakes no and again no no
again, and the women, they crush in closer,

to enfold the mother who lost you last night,
to press her brittleness back,
the women.

Hush now, but you were supposed to stay alive.
Your mother's loved *Kaddish'l*[1], you were meant

---

[1] Kaddish'l: endearing term for a son who will recite the prayer for the dead (mourner's Kaddish) upon his parent's death (Hebrew/Yiddish)

to be the one to stand in the pelting rain
skirring across the graveyard's sheeted ice,

and recite the way it should always have been:
when the mother goes, the son stands and recites.

Hush now, your mother hides a husk for a heart
and a stone sits deep where her soul once pulsed.

Listen now the silence, so loud and hard—
no echo struggles up through the snowy loam

that blankets your body so finally. No harm
any longer, finally. No harm no breath no laugh

no life. What version of sanity brings you so soon
to this quell of quiet, to this farewell place,

to the end of the world on a stillborn afternoon
in a whiteout blizzard as white as the shroud,

as numbing and raw as the spotless *tallis*[2]
embracing now your earthly remains?

Today they put you in the frozen ground,
a frigid trifecta for the meteorologists.

Snow. Sleet. Hail the almighty
storming spirit. We can hear heaven

pinging pinging ice pellets of shock
onto the wooden board that separates

---

[2] tallis: ritual prayer shawl (Hebrew)

your earthly remains, so recently quick,
from us who remain, stunned, on the earth.

We the women who remain on the earth
remain standing, shuttered and stooped

around your huddled mother, double-bent,
fending off the great wingèd capes

of the vulture umbrellas clustered like shadow
angels of death gently nudging our shoulders,

reminder of how feeble is the attempt
to hope and hide and shelter in place.

A mother of five is always counting heads.
Leaving your grave, counting heads. One

gone missing. She worries you'll be cold,
you're way too skinny, she never liked the sound

of that cough and you, you refused to eat
the healthy stuff. So hush now, hush.

Your mother will survive you, bleeding inside,
by counting heads. Four remain.

I Consider Forty

I consider forty. Invisible.
      I reconsider forty, in light of forty-five.
I remember thirty, vaguely.
          I forget eleven, probably for good reason.
I consider aging something to be done well.
      I reconsider, endlessly, the art of being female.
I remember the girlish charm of my childhood.
        I forgive my mother for trying to frown it out of me.
I reconsider my sister's attitude, the altitude of her moral perch.
      I forget those hours we played together as equals.
I consider my daughters, their fleeting girlhoods.
      I reconsider my preference for raising sons.
I want to forget my panic at discovering a penis on the ultrasound.
      I remember wishing it would magically melt away.
I remember my last was the hardest pregnancy of all.
      I forget the miserable infancy of my first born.
I reconsider motherhood, a quarter century after my start.
      I forgive my husband his wooing me for just one more.
I consider family, and my own place in the orbit.
      I reconsider forty: birth as proof
                          that I exist.

He Wonders What It's Like to be Pregnant

My pants look quite normal 'til you get to the belt.
The elastic stretches wide so two can fit in one,
marking a welt cinched beneath my bulge—
      (you know how you feel when you overindulge?)
Think of me as a man with a prominent beer belly.

My bladder calls for attention by the hour on the clock.
I'm familiar with a map of every Starbucks within range.
Lines and locked bathrooms are the absolute worst—
      (you know how you feel when you just gotta go first?)
Think of me as a man with a maddening prostate problem.

My abdomen ripples with strange ebbs and flows.
Imagine being kicked, from the inside out,
by knee knobs, elbows, miniature heels—
      (the roil and heave…you know how that feels?)
Think of me as a man who eats Tex-Mex for breakfast.

In sum my breasts ache, nipples leak, hips spread.
My veins bulge, bladder seeps, feet swell, hairs shed.
Think of me as a man—

Oh, this entire endeavor is futile.
Don't think of me as a man at all.

you the shining thing

Meet me in the daffodils, that velvet field of sunlight.
Wear your braided necklace of hope and hazy dread.
Take this pipe and smoke a screen to shield us from their
prying.
We could be Victory winged, all marble veined and dead,
our gone heads with plaited locks
lazy maimed and
dying.

Dying
could mean freedom.
You could be a bell—you the shining thing.
And I the weather wounding you, whispering and flying.
I storm you sometimes. And I blow you sometimes and I sing.
And I wring you restless 'til the breath of you is borne, rendered airy
as a mockie's wing, secretive and torn. Even so I love your swells, your
shoulder dips, *ma belle*. Your hollow waist, your flaring mouth, your
beaded lip that's
lying.

Lying
could mean liberty.
I could be the bell, and you the gnomy hunchback
bending low into my tarnished coat, sucking dry my brassy womb
on cresting notes of sighing, rending me with loveliness, shy and slow
as lightning. My blood washed skirts, they float atop this bounded life
I know. I call you and I bawl until the clamor of me cracks and
writes a history of
crying.

Meet me where the golden vista meets our bellies, swollen.
Bind your wrists. Bind our breasts.
Grab your hair and shear it.
Bells we are, these shining things, divinely tuned, a-pealing.
Victory, her head forgone above the prow is kneeling.
She's woke. Unblessed.

Our time is chiming.
Go ungently.

And know that you can bear it.

The Women Are the Story

I surround myself with myself: dark goddess
in cloak of black with blistered voice
dares to speak a truth.

In the shimmer of a lake, a sudden halo reflects upon my head—
shudder shudder and sigh.
The gauzy aura drifts away,   air   echo   and nothing.
I dare to be gowned in black.

I am gorgeous to behold in glass. Each month a river bleeds
from me, each year a great heave and flood—
sucker of nipples, daughter, nymph.
Each newness less like new.

Of late my riverbed crackles dry—
a mariner's regret, and ancient.
Desiccated hairs, tangled skin, eyes suck
lips like creases of plums.

In the mirror surface of a still pool: a swell. Myself
emerges, in shroud of black and robe of white—
mound at birth, heap at death. I dare

To age,
       to speak a truth.
I dare to stay
       my seat.

First Date

Xander lounges easily in his deep velvet chair,
trousers just tight enough to suggest
the muscular thighs of a runner,
pinstripes just wide enough to be considered au courant.

In the dark smoky cellar of one of Manhattan's venerated after-hours establishments
I watch myself tuck the hem of my pleated skirt beneath my knees.
I watch myself smooth a stray hair behind my ear.
I watch myself sip my wine cautiously.
I'd only ever read about places like this but believe
this is something I could get used to.
Xander watches me fuss.
Prim, he decides.

What if he thinks I'm prim? I worry.

Xander is talking.
I tune in.
I could be good for you. In so many ways.
Intellectually, emotionally, financially, sexually.
Xander speaks with assurance.
I wonder if maybe he's right.

I lean forward on the bench.
Who are you, Xander?
Alexander? Xan? Alex?

Xander smiles smoothly.
For you, my dear, I can be all of those men.
Or if you prefer, I can be none of them.

East, Meet West

A half carafe of wine and the Ladino hum of *Adios Querida*
bring me back to the tall Sephardi with the bedroom

lashes and the lush dark curls and the single bougainvillea
blossom he left on my pillow after our midnight drive

up the Pacific Coast Highway, just an
east coast girl with a west coast hunger,

and from the wine drenched brink I teeter
on a toehold perilous and steep, lest I forget

that I accepted his *kiddushin*[1] after only eight
short weeks of red-eyes and sunshine and his children

and his ex, and what the wild
west coast can do to an east coast girl

---

[1] kiddushin: Jewish betrothal

An Unusual Collection

An unusual collection the visitors murmur with
a puzzled crease, *but what exactly are we looking at?*

Bits of string, buttons, green pennies and the occasional
stray Israeli shekel, ribbons festooned with
dried frosting, some giggles. The perfect ponytail.
A someday boy who'd bestow mystery kisses.
And don't forget the playing cards—
a Queen of Hearts, a Queen of Diamonds,
a future flecked with shards of relationships,
all taken from Bubby's little drawer near the stove
in secret, for keeps.

An unusual collection.
Bubby's bits of string became my baubles. I took
for keeps the forgotten things, the things
no one else wanted.
Bits of string, buttons, a drifter niece,
a handful of husbands. Apartments so bare
almost anyone could perish in them.

What you take for keeps no one expects you
to give away. Four husbands
equals three *gets*[1] plus one *kesubah*[2].
An unusual equation.
And don't forget the kids—
how do they all add up? A couple
of sons from this one and that,
plus the two daughters and don't forget
the stepchild whose emerald eyes
belong in another's face.
An unusual arrangement.

---

[1] get: document of divorce (Hebrew)
[2] kesubah: marriage contract (Hebrew)

Bits of string, buttons, an old glove,
a new husband. I took for keeps
the forgotten things, the things
no one else cared for. A lost nephew,
the lone beta fish that refused to die. Fridges full
of nothing and neighbors who knew
when to leave well enough alone.

An unusual collection the visitors muse
amazed, *but how on earth did she have the nerve
to marry then leave then marry again?*

The museum of husbands hosts
an unusual exhibit, where here one may view
pronouncements stamped and sealed
by rabbis and esquires—
twelve lines long—signed here—and there—
we now proclaim this erstwhile wife free
to curate an unusual collection,
teeming with tales and bits
of biography, the patina of the passed
and the music of memory.

The Secret Real Life of Anon.

Anon. keeps two collections of food in her pantry. The first is a neat cluster of energy bars, protein packets, kale chips, and coconut water. These are healthy choices that Anon. always keeps on hand to fuel her body, a fitness instructor's body. The second is a secret. It is a hidden hoard of extra-large bags of Cheetos, sticky caramels that pull up her dental bridge, and Halloween candy that Anon. has sneaked from her children's drawers while they were asleep. Anon. hides this pile so well that she sometimes can't remember, in the crazed scattered rummaging of a midnight binge, where on earth she might have buried her stash this time.

Anon. keeps two cabinets of spirits in her breakfront. One cabinet is for company. Whenever her husband invites his colleagues to dinner, Anon. trots out the chilled Veuve Clicquot, the Glenlivet and Johnnie Blue, and the Woodford Reserve if the guests are not that important. The other collection contains the same exact drinks, except these bottles are already half empty when no visitors are expected, and only Anon. knows why.

Anon. keeps two heaps of underthings in her closet. The neat pile of satin and sex and lace has remained, like its owner, untouched for years. The other mess is functional, pit-stained and frayed, and also resembles its owner in much the same way. At least this is how Anon. sees herself.

Anon. keeps two weekly appointments with her therapist. On Mondays they explore Anon.'s complicated relationship with food, with alcohol, with intimacy. On Thursdays Anon. talks out loud about overcoming her addictions, nods her head in all the right places, and makes appropriate eye contact with the therapist, all the while daydreaming about her upcoming weekend bender in minute detail.

Anon. keeps telling herself stories with happy endings.

Excess

When the world is too much with you the Cabernet comes in a box
        and you pop dry roasted almonds from the bottomless
Costco bag. Bigger is always better.

You're suddenly in your forties and your baby hugs you hard.
        All she seems to want is to crawl back inside you and reattach
the cord. Somehow her apple juice is now on your tongue.
        Sweet emotion.

You miss your thirties' thirst. What's poetic about a dozen years
        married? Unless you find he lied. The floodgates open wide.
Your daughter swings upside down and sings.

A trampoline is the perfect place to shatter an elbow or your heart.
        Baby girl, beware the big boys they will trample you. Baby
girl gives the best kisses. Hard to believe he needed to woo you
        with jewels for this one.

You pop another almond into your mouth, crunch. *Flick*
        goes the remote. The president tweets again. Unprecedented.
Dispense with the stunning already. Enough.

You find clever ways to disguise a daytime drink. Pour Stoli
        into the plastic mug announcing the name of your middle son.
Eventually he knows to ask before he sips. Refill with Advil
        to stave off morning's regret.

How much can a belly bloat? Unless it's a life—immeasurably.
        You wash your hands and your wedding ring slips.
Be thankful for leaps of faith and friends who dance.

The friends you meet and the ones you keep are entirely different.
        Like it's so easy to get married—you do it often. Harder
to stay in the boat than to rock it. A different captain
        for every ship.

You find a silver strand in the nest of hair. Blank in the mirror.
    You miss the catcalls of the past decade. Too many rejected poems, too many invisible glances.

Yank goes the lone white hair from your head. Two will now grow
    in its place, they say. Your married son is married now;
his wife pulls him far. Are you mistaken or is he leashed
        to her ring?

You rummage and binge 'til your gills turn green. Swallow.
    Your bearded father appears only to repeat—don't darken
my doorstep don't visit my grave. Be a different daughter.

No one does Yom Kippur like you: jet off to London, find a rabbi
    who'll do. Sip with pursed lips high tea at the Ritz, then atone.
Repent and rejoice. Fasting means purging at Fortnum & Mason,
    clotted cream, scones.

How many fitness classes can you sweat? Outrun, outdance,
    outlast your diet. Cami, vest, sweater, scarf. You layer
your love and undress at will. Your will. Not his.

You choose to wear the panties with the tear. Your bras are granny
    beige because who's looking anyway. Elastic threads trail
down your back; they tickle like a lover's lips. What is a yarn
    but a story unraveled?

Just in time your sweet youngest son charms you from the ledge.
    A stack of newspapers with screaming headlines molders
in the basement. The bag of nuts is still half full

and the White House still half empty. Bite down hard, this may hurt
    a bit. You run to the toilet and stick a finger down your throat.
Out with the bad.

The Big Top Comes Down: A Consciousness Poem

once the elephants left the crowds stopped coming to the circus but look do my eyes deceive me the elephants are back they are blustering along on Capitol Hill with old white-man creases leathering their skin leaving huge piles of shit in their wake for the humane rights activists to shovel and yes the crowds are back to see the gilded circus with their very own eyes especially the trumpeting elephants imported from Russia but the parks department submits based on alternative facts that it's not truly a crowd it's really fake news it's a scattered gathering of empty bleachers lining the parade mall of the grand old circus the greatest show on earth headlined by the triumphant return of the elephants their legendary memories faulty somehow remember last year how they snorted and swore and yet oh my god here's the winning new ringleader just promoted and he's tripping over the ludicrous length of his tie he used to be an ordinary clown y'know all he did was comb-over the orange wig and shift his makeup from white to perma-tan but some clowns are scary and this one likes water for his next trick he wants to pour gallons of it down Ahmed's gagging gullet oh yes he's a self-styled high inquisitor turned into a meme this big league circus ringleader oh look there he's cracking his golden pen now to tame the donkeys braying out of control in an obstinate corner of the congressional ring ladies and gentlemen hell is empty and all the losers are here the circus is not shuttered it's terrific it's tremendous just look at those asses their portfolios prancing ringing round the oval kicking up their heels amidst piles of rubles they imagine they're stallions able to vault a fantastic wall and see up there the amazing gymnastics of the aerialist acrobats wow they can twist themselves into anything huh the people on the pavement ooh and aah and scratch their heads as they witness hope and change swing upside down from filmy vows of lightweight silk and in the center of the platform can you see the monkeys tilting at that crumbling Mexican windmill or maybe it's Syrian who really knows and guess what my friend the great cats are back the pink pussyhats no more jumping through hoops or performance on demand hear those fierce felines roar they're swarming the parade route and chasing this circus act right out of town watch the ringleader ex-clown snatch a bellicose bow amid the hue and cry believe it or not a Ripley themed spectacle is playing itself out on the splendid stage of our nation's capital

Jessica Rabbit Plays the Piano

At the Philharmonic on a Saturday night. Brahms
Trills to life at the flight of her fingers. Air becomes breath
                Beneath her nimble run. *Maestoso*.

The maestro commands. First movement majestic.
Jessica Rabbit, a scarlet woman

At the Philharmonic on a Saturday night. Less of a dress
She's painted on red, fine black hair bobbed chic
                And torrid. Swelling violins

Surround the sound of the Steinway
She tames with her golden stiletto. *Adagio*…

The concerto slows. Down, boys.
Jessica Rabbit sits sculpture-still perched
                At the bench, pert nipples like satiny cherries

Beckon in the gleam of the polished piano face, as if to flirt
"My fingers! Down there!" *Allegro non troppo,*

The composer cautions. Is it my imagination
Or is the audience tonight tumescent in anticipation
                Of an explosive surge up the keyboard? *Forte!*

The composer commands, and Jessica Rabbit's rippling naked back
Composes a paean that makes you just want to rude

Her breathless. When Jessica Rabbit finally rises,
Finished, with a staggering flourish, all the tongues
                Wag at the triumph of her electric *tremolando*

While all the eyes fix on the twin whorls of wet
That had streamed from her thighs during the ferocious recital.

How vital. Those pools of sweat, staining her bottom
In thirsty claret spills that beg you to lap them.
                    Look at her! Or listen. Jessica Rabbit's sizzling *glissando*

Mocks the god of effort with sweeping insouciance,
And melts the ivories into reverent surrender.

Deborah Kahan Kolb was born and raised in Brooklyn, NY and currently lives in the Bronx. Much of her writing reflects the unique experiences and challenges of growing up in, and ultimately leaving, the insular world of Hasidic Judaism. As a single mother, Deborah earned her BA and MA degrees in English/Creative Writing from CUNY Queens College, where she served as editor of the Queens College Journal of Jewish Studies and was the recipient of the James E. Tobin Poetry Award, the Lois Hughson Essay Prize, and the Essay Prize in Holocaust/Genocide Studies. She earned her MS in School Administration and Supervision from Touro College, after which she served as principal of a private school for disadvantaged children of Central Asian descent.

Her work has appeared in numerous online and print publications and has been selected as a finalist for the Anna Davidson Rosenberg Poetry Award and an Honorable Mention in the *Glimmer Train* Fiction Open. In 2018 Deborah was a recipient of the Bronx Council on the Arts BRIO Award for poetry, and her debut collection, entitled *Windows and a Looking Glass* (Finishing Line Press, 2017), was a finalist for the 2016 New Women's Voices Chapbook Competition. Deborah is the producer of the short film *Write Me*, adapted from her poem "After Auschwitz." Read more at www.deborahkahankolb.com.

www.ingramcontent.com/pod-product-compliance
Lightning Source LLC
LaVergne TN
LVHW041553070426
835507LV00011B/1070